A Carpe

TOOLS

by Michèle Dufresne

Pioneer Valley Educational Press, Inc.

Look at the carpenter.

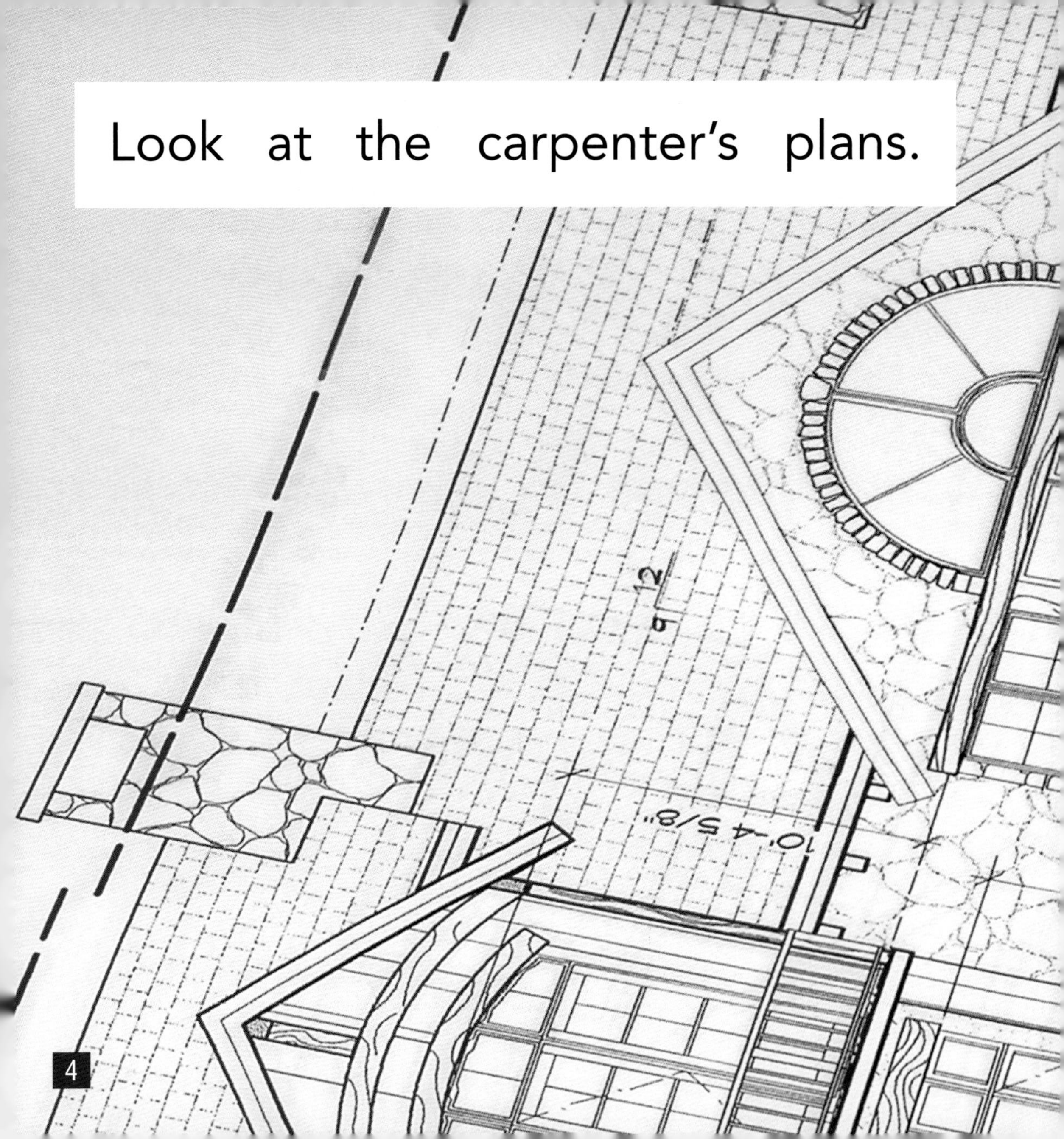

Look at the carpenter's plans.

Look at the carpenter's toolbox.

Look at the carpenter's pencil and measuring tape.

The carpenter is measuring the wood.

Look at the carpenter's drill.

The carpenter is drilling a hole in the wood.

Look at the carpenter's hammer and nails.

The carpenter is hammering the nails.

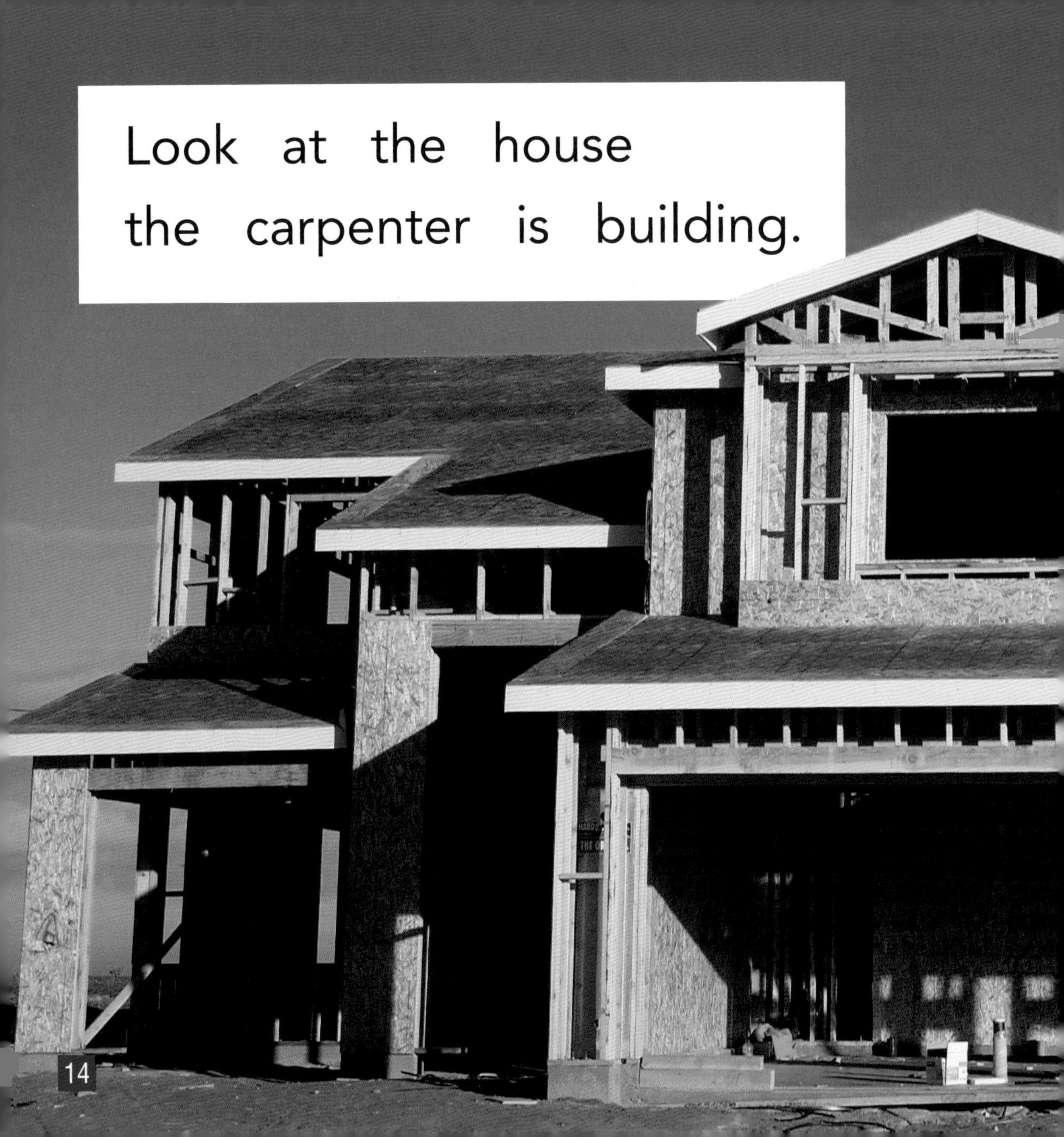

Look at the house
the carpenter is building.

A CARPENTER'S TOOLS
drill
hammer
measuring tape
nails
plans
pencil
toolbox